Fire in My Head / Flame in My Heart

Poems for the Pyrocene

Fire in My Head / Flame in My Heart

Poems for the Pyrocene

by

Ellen Girardeau Kempler

© 2025 Ellen Girardeau Kempler. All rights reserved.
This material may not be reproduced in any form, published,
reprinted, recorded, performed, broadcast,
rewritten, or redistributed without
the explicit permission of Ellen Girardeau Kempler.
All such actions are strictly prohibited by law.

Cover design by Shay Culligan
Cover image from the original, "After the Fire, No. 1, 2017,"
by John Pascoe, used with permission from Pascoe Studios
Author photo by Lexie Agauyo

ISBN: 978-1-63980-713-0
Library of Congress Control Number: 2025933221

Kelsay Books
502 South 1040 East, A-119
American Fork, Utah 84003
Kelsaybooks.com

Acknowledgments

Thanks to the editors of the following journals where some of the poems in this book first appeared, sometimes in slightly different form:

The Dewdrop: "Jet Lag (After Seeing the Prehistoric Paintings in Pech Merle Cave)"
Narrative Northeast: "Bones"
Orange County Writers Anthology: "Dog Dream in Drought Time"
The Rising Phoenix Review: "Darwin's Garden," "Blue Cut Blues"
Tiny Seed Literary Journal, Poetry of the Wild Flowers Anthology: "Fairy Slippers"
Tiny Seed Literary Journal: "Fire Drill (Santa Rosa, California, 2017)"
Water Book, Poetry Forge: "Thirsting," "Transcending"
Wild Roof Journal: "Necklace of Names (Necklaces of Islands)," "Apparition"
The World in Words: Laguna Beach Library 13th Annual Poetry Contest: "Southern California Saint" (Adult, First Place)
Writers Resist: "Elegy at the End of a Beach Walk"

Contents

1. Thirsting

Zero Hour, Hawaii-Aleutian Standard Time,
    August 8, 2023   17
Fire Drill (Santa Rosa, California, 2017)   18
Darwin's Garden   20
Southern California Saint   21
Blue Cut Blues   22
Dog Dream in Drought Time   23
Wishing for Fall (Southern California, 2020)   24
Poem Ending with a Line by Robert Frost   25

2. Mourning

Wing Section (Latitude 33)   29
Buckets (Laguna Beach, California, Winter 1998)   30
Necklace of Names (Necklaces of Islands)   31
Because, Bambi   32
When the Deer Were Here   33
Carpe Névé   34
O Moon   35
Elegy at the End of a Beach Walk   36

3. Coping

Beach Triage   39
Bones   41
Pandemic Time   42
Free Solo   43
Lockdown Haiku 1–5   44
True Religion   45
Earthworks   46
Almost-Spring Song   48

4. Transcending

Southern California Equinox	51
Fairy Slippers	52
Haibun from a Campground in the Path of Totality, August 21, 2017	53
Ecstasy	54
Eating the Harvest from Mali Ston Bay	55
Facts of (My Next) Life	57
Jet Lag (After Seeing the Prehistoric Paintings in Pech Merle Cave)	59
Apparition	61
Climate Notes	63

I went out to the hazel wood,
Because a fire was in my head
—W. B. Yeats, "The Song of Wandering Aengus"

The ideas explored here began to take shape during *Orion Magazine*'s 2020 environmental writing workshop, at the base of the remote "sky islands" of Arizona's Chiricahua Mountains. Sheltered out of time in that protective space, some 100 writers gathered in a kind of Earth grief summit. Coincidentally, this event happened in the world's last week of normalcy before global Covid lockdowns. Since then, we've witnessed one carbon-fueled disaster after another—disproportionately affecting the planet's poorest and most vulnerable people. Continuing record-breaking heatwaves, droughts, fires, floods, tropical storms, hurricanes, tornadoes, and landslides have brought the climate emergency home with frightening urgency. As an Oregon native, California resident, environmental activist, and global traveler, I've watched with growing alarm as the places I love have suffered from extreme weather and habitat loss. This book is dedicated to the writers (especially poets), artists, musicians, scientists, climate activists, and community leaders who've kept the green flame in my heart alive, and to my family, friends, and mentors for tending it. Thanks, especially, to my husband, Roger, and my daughters, Holly and Alex, who work every day to heal the world.

1. Thirsting

Denatured by heat we wilt—
skin peeling leathery leaves.
No buds or green shoots in our future.
So thirsty. Deep water me.

Zero Hour, Hawaii-Aleutian Standard Time, August 8, 2023

Wind propels fire fast past Front Street to Lahaina Harbor. Graveyard now.

Fire Drill (Santa Rosa, California, 2017)

At bedtime, no hint. Sky clear.
Moon rising. House built like a boat.
Wine Country hills a lullaby of waves.

Attachments spill from small rooms—
tatami mats, heirloom glass, a seventeen-
year-old cat. Broad decks echo parties past.

The retired couple thinks of other five-alarm nights.
Repeats these mantras: *Eleven miles is so far away.*
Smoke smell, no flames. No official order to get out.

When a daughter phones at 10 p.m., they pack,
then sleep, only to startle awake at midnight
with her second call: "You must leave NOW!"

Registering the red sky, siren winds, flickering
ridge, they start the car, drive fast downhill,
then meet a wall of flames. Turn back.

Back home, they place a panicked call to 9-1-1.
Dispatcher says, "GET ANYWHERE SAFE!" They run
to the pool next door. Balance on the edge. Jump in.

Gasping air through soaked shirts, watching the world
burst into flame, standing back-to-back, they ask,
How long does it take a house to burn down?

All night. The night they could have died.
Wind keening. Propane tanks exploding.
Timbers crackling. Air buzzing embers.

For six hours they hold each other. Shiver.
Cry. Think of family. Say, "I love you. I love
you. I love you." Miraculously, survive.

Pulling themselves out of the pool, they greet
the sepia dawn. Survey their home's charred ruins.
Grab hands. Walk away through smoke and ash. Go on.

Darwin's Garden

It is not the strongest of the species that survives . . .
It is the one that is the most adaptable to change.
—Charles Darwin

Here in my backyard
it's survival of the fittest.
Even the aloes seem to collapse
into themselves. Azalea buds darken
and drop. Camellias fail to flower.
Peach trees yield impotent fruit.
Leaves rustle like demand letters.
Branches rattle like percussive bones.

We count waterdrop coins—
filling basins, buckets, barrels—
harvest shower water before it heats,
sprinkle potted plants with half-drunk
thimblefuls of leaf-damp.

Just 150 years ago
prospectors sluiced snowmelt-streams
that rushed from high-Sierra vaults,
weighed the dust and nuggets,
then banked their wealth in cities,
spreading roots like weeds.

Those salad days
of gold and growth
now seem like green mirages
in this thirsty state,
whose promise wilts fast
in waterless waves of heat.

Southern California Saint

Airlifted from the Andes
the goatherd with a saint's name
is now patron of fire safety,
with two devoted herds
and one apostolate mutt.

Who else would have faith
that the tall sapless stalks
blighting these sunburned hills
would keep the bleating congregants
chewing down to flame-proof earth?

Among the brown ridges and boulders
the moveable flocks hunker down to feed
and breed, nimble, playful kids.

Safe behind coyote-proof fencing,
they will soon grow serious,
intent, slow to startle—
electric currents clicking as they work,
like rosary beads counting prayers.

Blue Cut Blues

There is more than one way to burn a book.
And the world is full of people running about with lit matches.
   —Ray Bradbury, *Fahrenheit 451*

In these drought-parched parts,
firefighters call the vegetation "fuel."
It might as well be kerosene,
carried on salamander trucks,
to ignite, then feed, the fire.

When wind and dry heat meet,
tinder and sparks conspire to burn,
driving forward in a whirling storm
through alphabets of subdivided streets.

Along the always-gridlocked route
to Vegas from L.A., the evacuees
stand still and silent—experiencing
the sear of ravenous flames.

Salamander suits protect us
from the truth: We will all
be climate refugees, drowning
in a rain of ash, choking on smoke
and our own denial.

Dog Dream in Drought Time

I dream the dog food keeps coming
day after day—large boxes
efficiently delivered
by quick silent men
driving fast trucks,
so fast that Arlo, our terrier,
does not bark until they're gone.

Box after box fills the front hall—
more than enough for him
and our two dogs past,
whose remains still haunt my closet

because I can't bear to unbox their ashes
and unleash them over the drab, thirsty hills
where we once watched them rejoice
in pure animal abandon—spinning
through mud puddles, careening
over green sports fields,

chasing the bright rain,
shaking the silver drops
into the wet
fragrant air.

Wishing for Fall (Southern California, 2020)

When heat and dry winds stretch into fall
I seek riparian dips where streams might run,
where I can imagine another kind of autumn,
nights chill enough to make brown thickets
blush, force burlap-dull brush into fiery riot.

As a child I dove into pond shallows on hot
days, skimming warm surface, then sinking
down toward cool mud bottom, hanging
weightless in murk, letting the cold-spot
poultice settle and soothe my skin.

Hike-diving now through shimmering
heat, I sink into the shady hug of hills,
grab my water bottle and rest in brief
relief, bottomless thirst quenched for once,
stilled by a strong urge to grow roots here.

Even this canyon escape is a warming place,
a cold-spot mirage I can't wish into oasis.
I stand, then slog on up through smoky air
and fire-season glare. This is fall now—
refreshment-free.

Poem Ending with a Line by Robert Frost

Fire lived in lightning
before human ancestors
carried embers back to their camps
to start the first cooking fires,
lure their kind down from trees,
warm icy nights, frighten beasts
and spirits, illuminate dark pathways
and make their meat digestible.

Over centuries we discovered
how two stones sparked.

In caves, reindeer-fat lamps
lit our handprints and paintings
and symbols, animating walls
with flickering light.

We offered the fire gods food
and gold and bodies. Soon
we began to sacrifice forests,
then turf, then coal,
then gas and oil.

The gods delivered smoke
and pollution, melting glaciers
and rising oceans, crop failures
and starvation, resource conflicts
and forced migration, drought
and flooding, ocean warming
and coral bleaching, heatwaves
and blizzards, wildfires
and extinctions.

The flames we first kindled
will draw us closer.

Some say the world will end in fire.

2. Mourning

Earthshell will crack
with urgent chick-taps.

This is not Ostrich Time.

Only birdbrains support an economy of excess—
coal mines, pipelines, consumption with no limits.

The Eagle cannot land in severe weather events:
snowpocalypse, polar vortex, thundersnow,
ground blizzard, super typhoon, bomb cyclone,
bombogenesis, microburst, macroburst, flash flood,
atmospheric river, waterspout, supercell, superstorm,
storm surge, sunny day flood, derecho, firenado

Wing Section (Latitude 33)

In the brightening garden
the male crickets begin—

serenading slowly at first
then faster, warming up

degree by degree, the flat
edge of one wing bowing

against the barbed edge
of the other, each wing-

pair lifting like a violin
in rising refrain, joining

each bow stroke together,
calling, courting, heralding

summer heat's arrival in
the still-December dawn.

Buckets (Laguna Beach, California, Winter 1998)

We had just moved into the Migraine House—its red-
flocked wallpaper's bordello vibe, white shag carpet
stinking of cat piss and sweaty squeeze of humidity
vise-pressures on my brain. El Niño rains began soon after—

eight inches in one day, then storms again for weeks,
overflowing drain channels, closing highways and streets,
flooding downtown shops, cutting the lights. Our old roof
hemorrhaged leaks. Buckets and more buckets caught

the obvious drips. The rest flowed in subterranean
streams through decks, ceilings and walls—blooming
musty damp. One night while we slept, a mud river
roared into the canyon below, carrying boulders,

houses, electrical poles and people in its wake. Local
lifeguards dove in, paddled through liquid dirt, followed
trapped residents' screams, wrenched open debris-blocked
doors, even lifted a baby to safety, hand-over-hand.

Two died in the end, a dozen homes destroyed. Watching
on national news, family and friends called, wondering
how we were. Still tracking the deluge, we said that
our buckets were holding, that for now, we were fine.

Necklace of Names (Necklaces of Islands)

A favourite reef, a beloved atoll: Marshall Islands parents name children after vanishing landmarks.
—headline from an article by Pete McKenzie,
The Guardian, March 23, 2023

You are the newest Atlantis, or should it be Atlanti? Because there are many, many of you sinking, drowning, pulling your living ballast down with you—your once-lush Edens already disappearing in extreme tides. You, Marshall Island children, named for submerged reefs, coves and peninsulas, will carry our map's lost places, lifting them like shipwreck treasures with the winch of your lives in other drier places—new islands rising like Pele's Hawai'ian necklace as Mauna Kea's undersea lava flows grow and cool, waiting to be mapped, explored, celebrated and (yes) even mourned in their time, their mythic beauty like your own lost-island places, like your own names—unheeded warnings we once launched like paper canoes in a Category 5 hurricane.

Because, Bambi

Because you saw the movie as a child,
and cried when Bambi's mother died.

Because you watched the zoo's fat polar bears,
witnessed their wild kins' emaciated, exhausted
survival struggle—once-fearsome hunters
unable to adapt to sea-ice melt.

Because, in Australia's bushfires,
koalas combusted like deadwood.

Because, elephants, killed
for bankable ivory tusks.

Minke whales, songs silenced
for blubber (hot-dark blood
flooding frigid bays).

Orphaned orangutans'
round-eyed surprise
to find their treetop nests
demolished by loggers.

Regal rhinos left mutilated,
holes in place of horns.

Because
this streaming snuff film
is a nature documentary.

Because
we can't turn away.

When the Deer Were Here

I tracked them, bite by bite,
past decapitated roses
and severed geraniums.

One summer before dawn,
a dog-walker spied a stag
knee-deep in vines, helping
himself to our tomatoes.

That good year for gardens
and deer, we often spotted
them in dance lines—trotting
out of the wild hills, shimmying
through the drainage ditches, high-
stepping down the wide streets
to feast at suburban smorgasbords—
all they could eat.

Then the deer disappeared in a long drought,
making our town's *Caution! Deer Crossing*
signs moot, my gardener's grumblings, mute—
sick jokes for mornings I harvest all they've missed.

I thought two rainy years
of bumper crops
would tempt them back.

Carpe Névé

Névé (n): A field of granular snow, especially the kind that forms on the surface at the upper end of a glacier.
—Merriam Webster Dictionary

If it snows, go
up to meet it
at its source—

the sky, wider
than the Arctic
winter, where

falling-star flakes
form, then spin,
landing lightly,

blanketing our
world in wonder-
ful silence, still

enough to hear
Earth's stricken
winter-heart

beating—steady,
loud, urgent as
a million wings

lifting in V-
formation,
taking flight.

O Moon

O moon so luminous
from Earth—our precious
water world—tragic, fragile,
an imperiled pale blue dot

in black space—prognosis so
bleak, there might be no saving
grace, only a chance to slow
the dying. We can't restore it

to its preindustrial state,
or return to garden bliss—
the time before we learned
to face our fatal flaws, to know

deep grief—this too-large loss,
this globe-shaped ache, this keen
longing for our ancestral home,
our Goldilocks planet as it was

when *Homo sapiens* first evolved,
a temperate world of just enough,
a place just right for life to thrive.
O Moon so luminous from Earth,

I fear forced exodus beyond your light,
our world a plague of heat, fires, drought,
blight, storms, floods—a drowning ark—
our cargo doveless, dockless, doomed.

Elegy at the End of a Beach Walk

(after "The Second Coming" by William Butler Yeats)

Heat buffets us seaward.
Sunburn sends us home.

We trail wakes
of bags and butts
clamshell packages
and coffee cups.

Styrofoam seeds
sprout like alien plants—
neoprene petals
band aid leaves.

Straws take root
in tangled kelp.

Saltwater and sun degrade.
Waves and currents take away.

Great Garbage Patch.
Undersea pyre.

Microplastic harvest
fills the widening gyre—
turning and turning
in the trash-dimmed tide.

Things fall apart.

3. Coping

Only practice this—
opening like bloom to bee,
unfolding like petals to sun,
burrowing like a worm into earth.

Beach Triage

First, the worst—styrofoam
chunks, unrecyclable,
      ready
to explode into shrapnel—
an uncountable number of
tiny, buoyant balls looking
to my fisheye vision like
armed food pellets,
      ready
to be carried by tides into
deep water, to float, plankton-
like through kelp, to be eaten
by some poor grouper, or even
a baleen whale, to sit in tender
stomach lining, an arsenal,
      ready
to detonate, joining plastic
bags, earplugs, candy wrappers,
cigarette butts and lighters,
drink bottles and caps, solo
shoes and socks, coffee stirrers,
dirty diapers, used condoms,
bagged and unbagged dog poop,
straws, broken boogie boards,
ripped rash guards and wetsuits,
sunscreen, sunglasses, swim
goggles, fins, surf wax, cans
and bottles, tooth flossers,
lip gloss, hair ties, sand toys,
half-eaten cartons of junk food,

cups and lids, phones, lighters,
receipts, coupons, gift cards,
balloons and ribbons—
       ready
and waiting for me at the ER door.

Bones

(for John Abbot Gardiner)

When a beloved dies
we gather like elephants
to mourn the bones—
touching each foot,
ankle, femur, rib,
vertebrae, shoulder,
stroking the pelvis,
jaw, cranium, moving
each one separately
with our trunk-fingers
as if by memorizing
and lifting each one
we could reanimate
body, spirit, self.

Pandemic Time

I trace chalk outlines
of gone-people
I have loved too long.

Warm air fills my grief-balloon.
I watch it rise
lift
separate us at last.

Because I am glad they are not alive for this
Pandemic Time.

With beach lots closed,
I park illegally and hike
down to the sand, to watch
how the world eerily goes on
without us—

our old perceptions suddenly distorted
by the strange—the rare sight

of a solitary black cormorant
standing like a statue on a rock,
great wings stretched wide to dry—

the surprising pile up of red tuna crabs I take for dead

before one raised claw signals
life goes on.

Free Solo

Pandemic walk
means following faint trails,
losing track of time.

I stop to watch a snail cross a crevasse
from park bench to weed patch.

One foot does all the work,
muscling out from the whorled shell
to stretch, pull across, then angle up.

Like fingers seeking rock holds,
four tentacles test air, sensing
the leafy bivouac ahead.

Summiting occurs at snail-speed.
Premeditated, steady—
the opposite of leaps
and bounds.

Lockdown Haiku 1–5

Last weekend's beach walk—
now forbidden. Postcard time:
Wish I could be there.

Kind of blue, kind of
jazzy. Bright notes light dark days.
Improvise times past.

Shelter in nature.
Let love open skylights. Look,
you can't cancel spring.

Coyote alert.
Listen. Join the yip-howl choir.
Celebrate the pack.

Name your pleasure boat
Resilience. Plan to ride
in any weather.

True Religion

I preach a sermon steeped in compost,
the forage & glean of earthworms,
the chomp & lace of moths & mealy bugs,
the slow slime of snails oozing through leaf mold,
the gnaw & trundle of tree rats carrying figs,
their droppings a trail itself compostable—
every rodent pellet, peel, pod, seed, bud,
flower, fruit, leaf, skin, going back to earth,
fermenting into a rich, steaming stew—
this religion a resurrection.

Earthworks

My spring garden is the scene
of ongoing earthworks, excavations
of the gopher and canine kind, discoveries
that emerge with the first light,
when the pup and I wake
and walk outside.

Every morning now
there's a freshly heaped pile
of fragrant brown soil
in my diminishing *Dymondia* patch.
Immediately, the dog digs in—
burying his nose, then diving
into the mess with his two front paws.
Dirt flies everywhere, and there is no end
to the new mounds, the wild digging
and the fruitless following. Meanwhile,
the gophers sit snug in their network
of hidey holes, stomachs stuffed full
of severed roots and a few yellow flowers.

When my youngest daughter was six
we stood in an upstairs bedroom,
gazing down at the same garden
in speechless and horrified amazement
as the just-blooming tulips I had lovingly
planted along the fence line vanished, one
after another, into the earth. I remember

glimpsing the furtive faces
of those rodent marauders popping up
to steal the first signs of spring,
bundling them underground like Hades
abducting Persephone.

That was the last time I planted tulips,
the very last time I tried to fight
the insatiable greed of gophers
at work.

Almost-Spring Song

The kingbirds are back to swaying
on improbably unbending stalks.
Hollow-boned, they float

songs like dandelion seeds
winged hopes buoyed
by warming winds—

lifting heavy hearts
leavening weighty occasions
rising above half-lowered caskets—

feathery flutter of souls
escaping into borderless
bright-blooming meadows.

4. Transcending

Say I eat the raspberry jam without bread or a spoon—
jam for the joyous taste of it, a sticky-sweet rebellion—
celebrating summer's messy ripeness like a bear.
Licking my fingers clean. No holding back.

Southern California Equinox

(after Michael Longley)

Spring arrives as a flute-note—
a sudden trill carried on warm wind
a melodious invitation to accompaniment
from every incoming bird—
the sweetest song from the plainest wren
      perched tipsily on our chimney top
the raucous shouts of bright-feathered jays
      begging for peanuts on the garden fence
the predatory cries of circling hawks
      riding updrafts, spying gopher holes
the anxious mother quail's *chi-CA-go* calls
      from deep inside trailside brush
her cheeping chicks appearing and disappearing
      in wavering lines, crowned with tiny feather hats
all settling into march-step with the changing rise of light,
the sun growing more intense, mercury inching up,
each day a gradual shift that soon becomes
      a recalibrated sense of hope—
when cricket concertos yield to cicada buzz,
frog song gives way to parched grass-rasp,
the powdery scent of sagebrush takes winter's place,
making every animal forget
the silver arpeggios of rain,
the muddy squelch of wet.

Fairy Slippers

At ten, I discovered green-world wonders
in the forest next to my house—shoe-flowers,
size small-enough-to-fit-my-pinky.

Fairy slippers grew at crouching level,
bright magenta against kale-dark leaves,
rhubarb-red stems. *Calypso bulbosa*
orchids bloomed in Oregon shade,
made for a woodland ball.

Stepping deer-light through dogwood,
ferns and firs, I drank the dappled shadow,
breathed the moss-sap scent of spring,
kept Calypso's secret for myself.

Haibun from a Campground in the Path of Totality, August 21, 2017

In a fallow Oregon tulip field set smack in the path of totality, we sit unblinking on overturned paint buckets, wearing goofy certified eclipse glasses, focusing up, ignoring cramped necks as moon consumes sun—swallowing our orange star segment-by-segment.

Sepia seeps into day. Temperature drops. Breeze quickens. Birds, bees, crickets and cicadas switch sound OFF in the sudden night. Stars emerge.

Recalling a space launch, we count down: "T-minus ten, nine, eight, seven, six, five, four, three, two, one . . ." At exactly 10:18:01 a.m., all glasses lift off. Pandemonium erupts.

Behold! Briefly safe for bare eyes, the sun's flaming corona wreathes the black-hole moon—pulsing, flaring, gone too soon.

> Primal reaction—
> precious, brief totality.
> Diamond-ring effect.

Ecstasy

Like bottled lightning suddenly
uncorked, a live electric current
fizzes through my veins, arcs
from my fingertips, gyrates
into my hips & exits my lips
as a whirling dervish of whoops
I do not recognize as my own.

My voice meets a primal chorus
of blanket-wrapped travelers.
We all move organically, eyes fixed
on an oscillating fluorescent sky-
ribbon of supercharged ions & protons,
now green, now violet, now red,
now yellow, now a quick pink—

a spontaneous aurora borealis flash
mob, dancing into dawn together—
discovering Dionysus
one early spring morning
on a frozen Reykjavik field.

Eating the Harvest from Mali Ston Bay

Our group of travelers
relaxes at wooden tables
in a pine-shaded grove
while the oyster farmers
prep our meal—huge pots
of blue-black mussels.

Arriving first, tiny glasses
of grappa, strong & sweet,
for toasting—a *živjeli* before
the island stars arrive: farm-
fresh oysters, three per plate.
Not nearly enough for me.

Tipping each rough shell
into my mouth, I feel the
Baltic inlet we just crossed
by boat exploding like surf
spray on my tongue, salty
& elemental as the sea itself.

I sit next to a woman who
says she could never eat
oysters, even the rare, flat,
European kind served here,
found in only two places in
the world. I slurp her three

& wish for many more,
making do with mussels
& more mussels, steamed
with olive oil, herbs & wine.
We're told the mussels attach
& grow on oyster lines.

"Always more mussels
than oysters at harvest time,"
says the farmer's son. Dockside,
I gaze across the sunlit Bay
of Mali Ston, soaking in sated
warmth—stomach & spirit full.

Facts of (My Next) Life

Enough *Homo sapiens*. I'm done.

Here are the facts of my next life:

> I will emerge as *Chelonoidis porteri,* a giant Galapagos tortoise, one of 3,400 survivors on Santa Cruz Island.
>
> I will be a proud, female member of a critically endangered, but growing, population, the only wild tortoises of our kind, free-ranging and entirely protected.

More About Me:

> Even in uncommonly dry times I can survive one entire year without eating.
>
> Although I am terrestrial, I often seek out freshwater ponds and mud wallows.

My To-Do list:

> I will soak in warm water and sunshine.
>
> I will graze like a cow in lush grass, forests and scrublands.
>
> I will sleep in the shelter of rocks and giant daisy trees.
>
> After mating season, I will make my lumbering, yearly, one-week, three-mile migration to lay my eggs in dry lowlands.

What Makes Me Unique:

   I am a highly protected species of international concern. I live in national parklands, tightly controlled by the country of Ecuador.

   To visit me, you must have a trained guide.

   Scientists capture and protect my hatchlings from island interlopers—cats, dogs, fire ants and rats—for seven or eight years before releasing them into the wild.

   For me there is no future and no past, only up to 175 years of present moments.

   I am free of human concerns.

Enough *Homo sapiens*. I'm done.

Jet Lag (After Seeing the Prehistoric Paintings in Pech Merle Cave)

I wake out of context
in a place where hours
are porous as limestone
where, over centuries,
rain and icemelt merged,

carving valleys and coursing
through canyons. Some rivers
ran underground, some above,
forming caverns like cathedrals
festooned in glistening calcite—

water flows frozen in rock—
stalactites and stalagmites,
columns and curtains, shields
and even rare cave pearls.
Deep inside cliffs, water

created aisles and apses,
arcades and galleries,
vaulted ceilings and choirs—
prehistoric sanctuaries
with welcoming entrances

framed in extended ledges
offering open-air shelter.
There, fires flickered through
time, leaving their marks
in charcoal, carbon-dated

to the last Ice Age, linking
our epoch to theirs, leaving
traces like footprints leading
back into darkness still
illuminated with their light.

Apparition

Even an old rose,
long thought dead,
can return to bloom.

You size up
the gray wood
and study the green.

Then you stand back
to see the plant's ghost-
shape emerge like an apparition
from days you a dug a hole, sliced
through wrapping, freed and stretched
the roots around a mound of soil,
covered them with earth and compost,
then watered until the bare canes sprouted
and flowered. There are no blossoms now.

You conjure their phantom colors,
so real you can almost catch their fragrance
on the air—spicy, with a citrus twist.

The familiar flowers fountain
from tall bushes along a path
you've walked before. Dressed
in satin, you peer through a veiled hat,
shearing the best apricot roses
for your bouquet, with purple violets
and ageless sprigs of green.

Climate Notes

1. "Zero hour, Hawaii-Aleutian Standard Time, August 8, 2023"
   The 2023 Maui Wildfire destroyed more than 2,200 structures and caused about $5.5 billion in damage, according to the U.S. Fire Administration. Driven by high winds and fueled by unusually dry conditions and the spread of invasive grasses, the fire took just 12 hours to almost completely burn through the historic district of Lahaina, where more than 100 people died. The inferno also destroyed homes, businesses, and livelihoods, devastating a community with an economy almost completely dependent on tourism.

2. "Fire Drill (Santa Rosa, California, 2017)"
   This poem recounts how artist John Pascoe (who provided the cover image for this book) and his wife, Jan LeHecka Pascoe, survived the Tubbs Fire in October 2017. Burning more than 210,000 acres, the fire was one of the most destructive in California's history.

3. "Darwin's Garden"
   A February 2022 study published in *Nature Climate Change* and led by the University of California, Los Angeles (UCLA), found that the 22-year southwestern North American megadrought is the region's driest in at least 1,200 years. According to the UCLA Newsroom, "One of the primary reasons climate change is causing more severe droughts is that warmer temperatures are increasing evaporation, which dries out soil and vegetation." These kinds of conditions have prompted some California Department of Forestry and Fire Protection (CAL FIRE) officials to start referring to the state's fire season as its "fire year."

4. "Southern California Saint"
   Like other fire-prone cities, Laguna Beach, California, contracts with a company that employs herders from South America to supervise brush-clearing goats, moving them as needed to graze in areas of overgrown, undeveloped land. Invasive plants like black mustard (introduced by Spanish colonists in the 1700s) comprise much of the flammable overgrowth. Many environmentalists do not agree with this practice because grazing wipes out native plant communities that have adapted to fire. The only alternative is the expensive and labor-intensive option of clearing and removing invasive species by hand, which, because of environmental concerns, is preferred to eliminating them with herbicides.

5. "Blue Cut Blues"
   On August 16, 2016, the Blue Cut Fire burned more than 37,000 acres in Southern California's northeastern San Gabriel Mountains. The fire started on a day when the National Weather Service had warned of extreme fire danger, with temperatures near 100°F and winds gusting to 30 mph. The fire forced the evacuation of over 82,000 residents, burned 37,000 acres, and destroyed 105 homes and 213 other structures. Still, according to an August 18, 2016, article by Rory Carroll in *The Guardian,* ". . . many caught up in the flames have shrugged off claims that global warming is to blame." Before (but, especially, since) 2016 this kind of climate change denial (and anti-science rhetoric) has been championed by some politicians opposed to adopting green energy alternatives to gas and oil and performing adaptations for the future that they deem too costly.

6. "Wing Section (Latitude 33)"
   Since the 1800s, farmers and other weather-watchers have observed how counting the rate of male crickets' chirps-per-second can be used to roughly estimate the outdoor temperature. Like all insects, crickets are cold-blooded. Even at Southern California's latitude 33, it is rare for December's early-morning lows to rise above 55°F, the temperature at which crickets begin chirping. Their particular music is more commonly associated with late spring, summer, and early fall. According to the U.S. Environmental Protection Agency, however, the average winter temperature across the country has increased 3 degrees Fahrenheit since 1896. While all four seasons are becoming warmer, winter temperatures have risen the most overall.

7. "Because, Bambi"
   In 2024, according to the World Wildlife Fund, "Experts now believe we're in the midst of a sixth mass extinction. Unlike previous extinction events caused by natural phenomena, this . . . is driven by human activity, primarily (though not limited to) the unsustainable use of land, water and energy . . . and climate change."

8. "Carpe Névé"
   According to the National Snow and Ice Data Center at the University of Colorado, Boulder, "One of the most prominent signs of ongoing climatic change is that, with few exceptions, the vast majority of glaciers are shrinking worldwide . . . Glaciers around the world have retreated at unusually high rates over the last century. Some have disappeared altogether. Many more are retreating so rapidly that they may vanish within decades."

9. "Elegy at the End of a Beach Walk"
   "Microplastics in different forms are present in almost all water systems in the world . . . ," according to the Earthday.org website. "There is more microplastic in the ocean than there are stars in the Milky Way. By 2050 there will be more plastic in the oceans than there are fish . . .."

About the Author

Ellen Girardeau Kempler is an award-winning nonfiction writer, photographer, and poet whose work has been extensively published in print and online. In 2024, one of her poems was shortlisted for the Bridport Poetry Prize. In 2016, she won Ireland's Blackwater International Poetry Prize and honorable mention in Winning Writers' Tom Howard/Margaret Reid Poetry Contest. Called "a timely and powerful selection of climate poetics," her chapbook, *Thirty Views of a Changing World,* was published in 2017 by Finishing Line Press.

A 2021 recipient of a Fostering Creativity in a Time of Crisis Grant from the city of Laguna Beach, California, Kempler established a poetry trail through downtown. It features short poems by community members in response to public art. She helps coordinate the Laguna Beach Library's annual poetry contest and judges poetry submissions for Bow Seat Ocean Awareness Programs' annual international student scholarship contest.

With a master's degree in mass communication, she has over 25 years of professional public relations and marketing experience with museums, aquariums, botanic gardens, science institutions, and conservation organizations. An active supporter of arts, social justice, and environmental causes, she is a climate-conscious traveler who embraces culturally immersive adventures. In her writing practice, she follows the late poet Mary Oliver's "Instructions for Living a Life": *Pay attention. / Be astonished. / Tell about it.*

www.ingramcontent.com/pod-product-compliance
Lightning Source LLC
Chambersburg PA
CBHW031204160426
43193CB00008B/502